BANDA SINGH BAHADUR

The history of Sikhism is a history of heroism and sacrifice. There have been many great martyrdoms in the history of sacrifices. The life of Baba Banda Singh Ji holds a special place in the creation of history. Madho Das (Baba Banda Singh Ji Bahadur) who was once neglected by the world was living a life of Bairagi Sadhus in Nanded area. When Dasmesh Pita Sahib Sri Guru Gobind Singh Ji reached Nanded, he met this Bairagi Sadhu. He was using his power against innocent people. After meeting the Satgurus, Madho Das became a man and collapsed in the Patshah's sanctuary. Patshah Ji baptized him and made him Baba Banda Singh and sent him to Punjab by giving special responsibility to all under the mission of upliftment

 Baba Banda Singh came to the Punjab and reorganized the Sikh power and started a struggle against the Mughal rule. When Baba Banda Singh advanced with the organizing power of the Khalsa, the great pillars of Mughal power shook. The Mughal forces suffered heavy humiliation in the battlefield. The city of Sirhind, which had the stigma of martyrdom of the younger Sahibzada Baba Jorawar Singh and Baba Fateh Singh on its head, was completely annihilated and the Khalsa Raj was established by hoisting the flag of the Sikh state for the first time.

 The adjective Bahadur was added to the name of Baba Banda Singh. In the Khalsa Panth, this great general came to be known as Baba Banda Singh Bahadur.

Baba Banda Singh Bahadur was a man who was living a life of alienation from worldliness. He was living in the far south of his country. Guru Gobind singh ji's holy words and the touch of the sacred lotus changed the outlook on the life of Banda singh Bahadur. After receiving blessings from Dasmesh's father, he returned to the Punjab to quell the Mughal tyranny. First the village-Pundri gathered the Sikh power and then launched such attacks on the contemporary political monarchy that the great empire of the country lost its footing. In retaliation for the martyrdom of the Shahibzads, the first flag of the Sikh state was erected in the Punjab, the capital was made and the coin was introduced.

Although it did not last long before the Mughal Empire, the high spirits expressed by Baba Banda Singh Bahadur cannot be underestimated. This is the time of his victories and achievements His last days there were no less important. His martyrdom is a manifestation of the courage that only the Guru's Sikh can have.

As a child, Banda Singh's name was Lachhman Dev. He was born on Sunday (October 5, AD) in the village of Rajouri, Poonch (Kashmir). His father Ram Dev was a Rajput of Bhardwaj Goth and worked in agriculture. Like the people who were born in poor families and got publicity in the last days of their lives, nothing is known about Lachhman Dev's childhood. Like the ordinary boys of the village halvahs, his bones were healthy, passionate and hardworking. He was fond of hunting and horse riding.

There was not much education in Kashmir in those days From ancient times it was the property of Brahmins only. Even in the twentieth century The educational status of ordinary Kashmiris has not changed much. Apart from the Pandits, hardly any prominent Kashmiri scholar can be seen anywhere. The Poonch area was particularly backward. Therefore Lachhman Dev did not get any opportunity to get education. In those days, besides halwahi, youngsters were fond of hunting, horse riding, archery etc. So Lachhman Dev's inclination was also on this side but he was not very kind hearted. He had received some of these rites from his mother or father, which made him a little soft-hearted and emotional. His life that he was still young The first dramatic reversal took place in.

It is said that once while hunting, Lachhman Dev killed a deer The arrow hit. She was injured and fell to the ground.

When Lachhman approached Dev, he saw a dying deer and felt some pity in his heart but after that another scene had a profound effect on his mind. Making up his mind, when he tore the stomach of the slain deer to clean it, two children came out of it who died in agony in front of Lachhman Dev's eyes. This made his tender heart tremble and his mind became sour from hunting. The mind felt such remorse and disgust that the heart at once rose above the world and worldly life. Lachhman Dev was no longer a Rajput. The interest had turned to the worldly apostate saints. Although he was only about fifteen years old, he left his housework and started associating with the sadhus who used to come to Rajouri on their way to pilgrimage to Kashmir. Soon a man named Janki Prasad came to Rajouri on a pilgrimage. His teachings made Lachhman Dev such that he left home and became a disciple of Bairagi and joined the congregation and walked with him. According to the tradition of Bairagis, Janki Prasad changed its name to Madho Das. It has appeared in many places in the Bairagi congregation. According to AD, on the occasion of Vaisakhi festival of Sammat Bikram, his group reached Baba Ram Bamman's camp near Kasur.

Many other sadhus were also present. One of them was Ramdas Bairagi. Madho Das joined Ramdas's party here. For many years he accompanied them on pilgrimages. Once on the banks of the Godavari he visited Nashik and stayed there. The place of Panch-Vati was a source of special attraction for the solitary saints. Not only was the solitary and beautiful scenery captivating here but it was also a place of special significance for the ascetics as it was the abode of Sri Ram Chandra and Sita ji. It was here that Madho Das met Joghar Oghar Nath who was famous for his Ridhi Siddhi and Tantric education.

He became so fond of learning yoga and Jantar Mantar that he became an ardent devotee and devoted servant of Oghar Nath. He knew that service was the key to success. The service of the Guru was considered to be a special means for the disciple to acquire certain virtues or knowledge, especially from the ancient saints. At the end of Oghar Nath's service to Madho Das. The mind became calm and he forgave her the secret means of yoga and the secrets of magic. Now Oghar Nath was very old. The last days of his life were near. He was very happy with the service of Madho Das. So at the end of the day, he gave her one of his most valuable works of yoga. This is the story of Sammat 1 (year 2). Shortly afterwards, Jogi Oghar Nath passed away. Having thus become proficient, Madho Das set about setting up his own monastery and marched from Panchvati to Chudi along the banks of the Godavari. Madho Das fell in love with a beautiful place near Nanded and made up his mind to stay there. Some distance outside the city, he built his hut on a high place in the dense trees by the river bank and secluded it. Began to live the life of an ascetic. Gradually the movement of the afflicted and needy began, and his fame soon spread throughout the city and its environs through mantras. Some disciples also came and thus Madho Das's hut took the form of a good and good mind and his worship and thirst began to increase day by day. According to Tulsi Das, "Ko Janmiyo Aso Jag Mahi.

The Lord is not found. " That is to say, there is hardly a rare fortunate worldly person who gets sovereignty or attains Hukam, then some ego and arrogance does not arise in his mind. Madho Das was being lauded here and there as a Siddha Yogi. There were many disciples around for the service. With this, his ego got muscles. She began to grow and flourish. There must have been a sadhu from outside but the mind was not a sadhu.

He did not show humility. Along with the arrogance, there was also some fickleness. It was his hobby to humiliate the visiting saints instead of entertaining them with hospitality and sometimes he did not even hesitate to make fun of them. He had strength and courage but he was lost. It was an unfinished mine of ore, waiting for a chemical to separate it from the dirt by washing it in a kiln or with a mixture of chemical drugs and washing it and shining it. While waiting, his sixteen years passed in Nanded. At the end of the autumn of Bikram (AD), Guru Gobind Singh arrived there in the form of an armored, horse-riding, saint-soldier, He turned his back on the Panth Khalsa and directed them to serve the oppressed masses of the time.

In the days when Madho Das was living the life of a sadhu in the South engaged in Bairagi Yoga and Tantra, Guru Gobind Singh was waging a crusade against religious bigotry and political oppression in the Punjab. Aurangzeb's policy of making the accused a Muslim from the beginning was not successful. The Marathas in the South and the Sikhs in the Punjab stood up for the protection of the Hindu masses. In the last days of his life, the king was either beginning to see some of the bad consequences of his austerity measures or he was getting stubborn with age. Whatever the reason, Emperor Aurangzeb wrote a letter of acceptance to Guru Gobind Singh, inviting him to come to the South for talks. Guru Ji wrote his world famous letter 'Zafarnama' in his reply, in which he drew the attention of the king to the non-treatment of the people of the country and said that I have no other choice but to come to an end with the sword. I will still be present for the talks if the king visits Kangra pargana but the king was very old and weak now and his health was deteriorating day by day. Also, since Bhai Daya dingh, the bearer of Guru sajhib's letter, had not returned on time from the king and it was not known whether he had been able to meet the king and deliver the letter, Guru He decided to go south.

Guru Gobind Singh ji was still near Baghor in Rajputana when he heard the news of the king's death on 2 February 202 AD.

There was no need to go further. So they returned to the north. He had reached near Delhi when Prince Mohammad Muazzam, the eldest son of King Aurangzeb, requested for help. At the time of his father's death, the prince was on the north-western border. His younger brother, Prince Mohammad Azam, being close to him, disregarded the rights of his elder brother, ascended the throne and became king. Emperor Aurangzeb himself and his forefathers, Guru Gobind Singh and his elders, were staunch opponents and enemies of religion. The martyrdom of Guru Arjan and Guru Tegh Bahadur was the result of their cruelty but Guru Gobind Singh forgot all the old enmities. They did not want to avenge their grandfather's cruelty on their troubled prince. In the name of justice, they were ready to help Prince Mohammad Muazzam and sent three hundred horses in the battle between Agra and Dholpur near Jaju on June 2, 2013. In this battle Muazzam was victorious and he became the king of India under the name of Shah Alam Bahadur Shah.
The new emperor Bahadur Shah, through his Wazir Khan-khan, requested to visit Guru Gobind Singh.

The meeting took place on 2nd July. According to the royal custom, no one was allowed to go to the king in arms, but Bahadur Shah gave it to Guru Gobind Singh and gave him as a gift eight thousand incense sticks, feathers and caps. According to custom, the Siropa was to be worn only at the Darbar and only the religious leader of the government, Sheikhul Hind, was allowed to take the royal khilat from the servant. Bahadur Shah also bade farewell to Guru Gobind Singh as a religious leader. Guru sahib summoned a singh inside the court, near the king, and allowed him to carry the Siropa.

The idea was that he would return to the country soon. Some seem to have thought that they would reach the area of Kahilur, which was the city of Anandpur, but there would be a need for an armed Khalsa, so the order said, My order to Subat Khalsa is to reconcile with each other. When we come to Kahlur then Subat Khalsa weapons. It will be a pleasure to come and be present. "But Guru Sahib's conversation with the king is not over yet. The king had to move first to Rajputana and from there to the south. In the south, his younger brother Kam Bakhsh had raised the flag of rebellion. To bring the conversation to a conclusion, Guru Sahib accompanied him to the south so that the matter could be settled wherever possible. This long journey took ten months. The king because of his brother's rebellion ,He did not see his government firmly entrenched. Therefore, it was very difficult for him to accept any statement of Guru Sahib which would cause any of his rulers in the north-west to revolt and make a fuss. Kingdom for Guru Sahib too It was difficult to walk along the camp for eternity. As a result, talks broke down at Nanded and all efforts made so far were in vain. Now again there was no choice but to put his hand on the hilt of the sword. When the emperor prepared to cross the Godavari and move towards Hyderabad, Guru Sahib encamped at Nanded for a while. This is the last week of September. Here's to yourself Reunited with Bairagi Madho Das.

On his journey south, Guru Gobind Singh came across a monk named Madho Das, who was staying in Nanded from the Dadu-Panthi Mahant Jait Ram in the Naraina Nagar state of Jaipur, who was happy to subdue the visiting saints and guests with Jantar-Mantra. He had also treated Mahant Jait Ram badly.

So Mahant Jait Ram requested Guru Sahib to reach Nanded but not to go to Madho Das's camp but Guru Gobind Singh did not pay any attention to this. They were on the throne of Guru Nanak, who rose to prominence by forcing the erring, the deluded and the deceitful to go straight. Guru Gobind Singh also reached Madho Das's shrine one morning. Madho Das was not in the monastery at that time. Guru sahib waited for him on his bed, and his fellow mounted the pots and pans of meat for their langar. The disciples of Vaishno Bairagi did not like these things. They ran to Madho Das to complain about this strange guest. Madho Das was very proud of his directness. He looked down on everyone. He had subdued many saints. So when he heard the disciples' words, he became very angry and came to his camp in red and yellow. He felt humiliated by someone else's bed on his bed and in his camp He considered the religion to have been broken by the burning of meat.

As usual he tried to turn the bed upside down with the help of yoga force and subdued invisible heroes but no one appeared, all the jantar mantras failed and Madho Das got nervous. This type of drama, even if it has some effect on the weak mind of Chetak, does not work with their strengths. Guru Gobind Singh ji was a great soul, before whose eyes the eyes of the arrogant saint were lowered. Till today no one was standing in front of him but now he has fallen here by himself. He came with great rage and arrogance, to dominate the guest who came to the house, but as soon as he saw him, he fell in love, bowed his head in humility and proceeded to make a respectful request in the presence of Satguru Ji.

It was such a miracle that this arrogant and arrogant Bairagi fell at his feet with great humility and without any hesitation he was ready to become a Singh. Now with the touch of her feet, lightning flashed through her body and mind.

Guru Gobind Singh saw a shining spark in the soul of this young saint, whom he, by His grace, awakened by making a light. To transform Madho Das's changed mental state into a new one, Guru Gobind Singh at once made him wear the Bana of the armed Singhs and, according to Sikh custom, ordained Singh and changed his name. Most famously, he used the term 'Banda' for himself and that is the term Most historians use it as a name. Thus in the twinkling of an eye Madho Das Bairagi became another. He was no longer a Bairagi Sadh. He had become a ready-made Singh and a saint soldier of Guru Gobind Sigh. So he went with Guru Sahib to his camp and started preparing for his new job and war life.

Banda Singh's started his journey to the Punjab after taking the rites of Guru Gobind Singh, when the old Bairagi Madho Das became a new man by the name of Banda Singh wearing a steel kirpan and an iron bracelet in his hand, his shoes awoke. He, who had come out of the realm of life in fear of doing deeds, by the grace of SatGuru, has now returned to the struggle of national service. It did not take long for Banda Singh to become acquainted with the doctrines of Sikhism and the efforts of Guru Nanak and Guru Gobind Singh to make a nation of heroes out of the crumbling Punjab. Banda Singh was shocked to hear how Guru Arjan was tortured and martyred on the orders of Emperor Jahangir and how the idol Guru Tegh Bahadur was killed on the orders of Aurangzeb in exchange for preaching Sikhism. . He had seen with his own eyes the pitiable condition of the Hindu masses being trampled under the tyranny of the Mughals. Banda Singh's eyes filled with blood when he heard of the tragic deaths and his rage against the Mughal Empire flared up. It was during these days that a Pathan from Sirhind stabbed Guru Gobind Singh several times and wounded him. When the Guru's ongoing friendly conversation with Emperor Bahadur Shah and Wazir Khan, ruler of Sirhind, became alarmed when news of the valuable titles presented by the king in gratitude for the military assistance rendered by Guru Sahib on the battlefield of Jajo reached him. He was the greatest sorrow of Guru Sahib and the Sikhs. By his order the last siege of Anandpur fell and was destroyed and by his order innocent Sahibzada was martyred. Now he began to fear his own sins that if the conversation between Guru Sahib and the emperor was successful, it would not be to his advantage.

So it is known that he sent two men after Guru Sahib to get him killed before he returned to Punjab. The author of 'Chatur Jugi' Granth says that first they went to Mata Sundari Ji in Delhi and from there they went to the South. They are known to be the first acquaintances of Guru Sahib. Was found and there was no doubt about his intentions in the dera of Guru Sahib at Nanded. Later, Guru Sahib's eyes were opened and a nearby servant also fell asleep. Guru Sahib struck the killer with the kirpan he had before he could do it a second time and his other accomplice was chased away by the fleeing Singhs.
The news of this disastrous attack infuriated Banda Singh even more. His blood began to boil. Now it has become very difficult for him to remain silent. He asked Guru Sahib for permission to go to Punjab to destroy the tyrant Mughals and punish the miscreants for their deeds.

Thieves and looters were common in those days. As Banda Singh's wealth was spreading all over the area, these raiders also started circling around his camp The comrades beat him so badly that he never looked back. In this way he easily reached the area of Bangar. By this time he was walking quietly and not interfering in anyone's affairs but this could not last long. After all, it was to alleviate the suffering of those who came from the south. Hence, he could not bear to see their suffering in front of them, nor could he remain silent. | One day he learned that a band of looters was approaching the village where he was staying and that the people were fleeing to the forest in fear.

Banda Singh had killed them instantly. He did not tremble and trembled. Thinking that the disease of the cowardly Panchs would not spread to the entire population of the village, Bada Singh locked the Panchs in a room and marched with a small group of Singhs to fight the raiders. Banda Si ngh's sudden onslaught was so daring and fierce that the raiders fled in panic, their legs shook and they fled, leaving behind the last loot they had. Their leader was captured and anyone who came to rescue him was either killed in battle or ran away. Seeing this, the villagers were also encouraged and prepared to defend their village. Now Banda Singh released the Panchs from the barn and ordered them to pursue the bandits. What's more, the vultures also became lions and pushed the fleeing bandits to the neighboring village and chased them away. This noble deed of heroism was the beginning of the glorious and world famous life of this hero. With this, Banda Singh started getting applause from all around and wherever a village needed protection and protection from looters, people would come to them and complain. On the other hand, it also made a general announcement in the area that our service is there to protect and support the poor and helpless people from the tyranny of professional looters and tyrants. Foods We need nothing but milk, yoghurt, ghee. Come on! You too become Khalsa and we will make you the guardian of the country but when could this matter to the government Chaudhrys? At times, they even serve the government on the one hand, and on the other, they are the backbone of crooked landlords. They seldom think of the welfare of the poor.

So instead of serving the country in association with the Khalsa of the area, Chaudhary became his opponents and passed or complained to the government officials.

So much so that Banda Singh reached the pargana of Kharkhoda and passed the villages of Sehri and Khanda. He sent Hukamnamas of Gobind Singh ji and summoned him so that the Sarbat Khalsa would unite and put an end to the tyrannical rule of the ruthless Mughals. The Singhs who came with him from Nanded also sent many letters to the chiefs of the country in which they wrote that Guru Gobind Singh himself had appointed Banda Singh as Jathedar of the Khalsa and it was the duty of the Khalsa to come. Come together under his banner for the religious war. Thus the memory of Nawab Wazir Khan and his presenter, of the massacre of the Sahibzadas at Sirhind was once again revived . Just what was then, Preparations began among singhs.

On hearing the news of the gathering of the Singhs in this way, many Jatts of Bangar and Brar Singh came from the north. Although none of the Phulke Chaudharis could reach him but he did a lot of service with money etc. and many people came. Many robbers and looters also gathered in the hope of looting Guru-Mari Sirhind. There is a village called Slaudi near Sirhind. There was a Singh, Ali Singh, a servant of Nawab Wazir Khan. On hearing of the preparations of the Singhs against Sirhind, Wazir Khan called Ali Singh one day and mockingly said: I will erase the traces of those who have come here, so that the sons of the previous Guru can be found soon.

What was Ali Singh's response to this sting? He only said that if he is a complete Guru then come by yourself, you don't need to be invited. The rest is up to me, give me leave and pay the bill. When could the Nawab give such an answer? Ali Singh and his other comrades were immediately ordered to be imprisoned in boats by boat, but it seems that in those days getting out of prison was as easy as being thrown into prison. Singh somehow slipped out of the jail and read the letter and reached Banda Singh. He was presently in the village of Sehri Khanda in Kharkhoda Pargana. The Singhs requested what was the matter now. Play the march drum and do the work. Banda Singh further replied that Hukamnamas and letters have been sent to the Singhs, they are coming from a distance, I want to join them, that is why I am waiting. It was recently reported that a large number of Singhs from Majha and Doaba had reached Kiratpur across the Sutlej, but the Pathans of Malerkotla and Ropar had stopped them. These Singhs have reached here after a long journey and now with the stoppage of Kiratpur the cost of the journey is getting harder,

 but Here Pishora Singh and Kishora Singh Arora traders have set up langar and are also paying some expenses. On hearing this, Banda Singh sent word to them that as long as no other message reached you from here, you should remain there.

Within a few months, Samana and Sadhora, Banda Singh had a large number of enemies who had a burning desire for war in their minds, and their faces were red with the taste of victory and martyrdom. Ali Singh and Mali Singh, who had come from Sirhind, one day requested that the Singhs who were to come had arrived, so that the expedition should not be delayed any longer. Banda Singh replied, "At present only those Singhs are waiting who are being called and who are coming from far and wide." After some deliberation it was finally decided that it was not proper to delay too long and the Khalsa should rush to start its work. As soon as the news of the ascent reached the Singhs, the Singhs would arrive with long and sharp midwives. So Banda Singh marched towards Sonipat with five hundred Singhs.

Sonipat is a very old town. At that time it was very strong and could withstand the army in greater numbers than Banda Singh's comrades. Could not even fully prepare. From then on, Banda Singh attacked with such force that at first the Dracula Cowards lost their footing and they fled the field and the faujdar ran towards Delhi. This victory raised the spirits of the Singhs. Man in the Malwa region

Singh's main intention was to kill Sirhind but Sirhind was a very large and lofty place. The faujdar here, Wazir Khan, was an outspoken Mughal chief.

Sirhind had a large army of its own and could carry a considerable amount of aid from all around. Banda Singh's advice therefore was that before attacking Sirhind, his right and left arms should be broken so that he could not receive any help from either side. With this idea in mind, Banda Singh first decided to modify the equation.

When Singh reached near Kaithal, he was informed that an army contingent on its way to Delhi was stationed at Bhune village. It turned out to be a good opportunity to meet the cost of muscle and Banda Singh took full advantage of it. He hurried to the corner and snatched the goods from the treasury guard. When the Hindu Amil of Kaithal came to know about this bandh of Banda Singh, he

The cavalry arrived on the scene with a police squad. Banda Singh's Companion Singh Most were pawns. So they hid behind the walls of the old house in search of a better opportunity. When the stakes were high, they jumped out of the holes and fell on the horses. Amil fell into the hands of the Singhs and his comrades fled. Banda Singh agreed to release him on the condition that he hand over all his horses to the Singhs. He gladly agreed. Banda Singh gave him permanent residency there on behalf of the Khalsa and appointed a detachment of Singhs there to settle the matter.

Loot

Banda Singh was very generous with what he came across Divided into peers. This convinced everyone that their heroic leader had no personal interest in the task.

Although these early malls of Banda Singh may have been very small and modest, they were very encouraging. Now he climbed straight to the front.

The martyr of Guru Tegh Bahadur in Delhi was Syed Jalaluddin, a resident of Samana and the Sahibzada in Sirhind. Executioner Shashal Beg and Bashal Beg was also the same.

As the killing of those who refused to accept Islam was considered a religious service of Islam, only the Sayyids deserved the honor of this service. That is why religious executioners were Syed. Samana was the wealthiest city in the area and it was thought that the plunder would ruin the whole area and would not dare to confront any other big city and the other would get so much money that it would cost the next campaigns. Will be easier. The Samanas were inhabited by the wealthy and high-ranking dynasties of Syed and Mughals. Twenty-two of them were rich men who had the power to come and go in palanquins. The coat of arms around it was like a fort, and every large mansion inside was a fort. The faujdar here was confident and encouraged that he would be able to fight any out-of-town attack from any angle and even if there was a siege no enemy would be able to enter due to the strength of the coat and failed to carry the Dera flag but Will be forced. Therefore, he did not pay any attention to the news of the invasion of the Singhs. He thought that the clumsy companions of Banda Singh did not suffer a single blow from the tangled antimony moguls of Samana but he came to know about it when suddenly Shooting from the other side, Banda Singh and his companions broke through the city from all sides and entered before they could close the gates. For hours, swords were brandished in the markets and streets of the city, and in the gutters. During this attack some robbers also entered the city following the Singhs. While Singh was searching the houses of Syed Jalaluddin and Shashal Beg, Bashal Beg, etc., while the looters were searching for the treasures of Samana Faujdar and other great Mughals, the looters got busy. Many of the great Mughal emperors closed the gates of their mansions and started setting fires inside, but they could not stay long in the face of the raging fires of the surrounding villages. These rich people owned land and were suffering from atrocities.

 So they were scrambling to get rid of their new and old worms. Eventually they started setting fire to the mansions which were very difficult for those hiding inside to fight. For them there was the fire of hell inside and outside the spears of the enemies and their own great sins on all sides surrounded them and pushed them to the brink of death. In this way, before nightfall, the high towers and palaces of Samana collapsed, which could not be restored to its former glory. An estimated 10,000 people died in the cyclone, most of them Syeds and Mughals, and many of those who survived were left forever.
The courage and bravery shown by Fateh Sigh in this attack had a profound effect on Banda Singh's mind. The credit for Samana's victory went to him. Banda Singh was pleased and appointed Bhai Fateh Singh as faujdar of nine parganas under him. Although Cable had won earlier, historians have called Samana Banda Singh's first victory. That's fine too. Kaithal was neither a very strong and strong place nor was there any confrontation that could be given a historical feature! Samana was a stronghold of the Mughals and of the Sayyids, which was broken by the Singhs and the backbone of the Mughal Empire in the Malwa was shaken.
Band singh generously gave Maya and goods to his fellow Singhs on this victory. At that time the Singhs had no paid army. Most of them had gathered with the spirit of love and service of the Guru Panth, not out of any greed but in the plunder of Samana where the Singhs got their share of wealth, they also accumulated expenses for the next campaigns.
When the news of the capture of Samana Par Singh reached Sirhind, Wazir Khan, the ruler of Sirhind, became alarmed. News was flying that Singh was about to return.

When Banda Singh and his companions reached Sirhind but wondered what he would do with this city, his whole body would tremble and his own sins would frighten him. There was a man. He made all the preparations to strengthen Sirhind and sent spies to ascertain the strength of Banda Singh so that in every possible way, efforts could be made to avert the impending calamity. Banda Singh, on the other hand, was no less vigilant. He had ordered that whenever an intelligence detective was found, he should be arrested and produced. Two detectives were caught. Taking one ear and the other. The two parted ways and were released on the orders of Banda Singh to go and give a message to Wazir Khan to get ready. Banda Singh stayed for a short time. His intention was to go to Sirhind as soon as possible but he also knew that Nawab Wazir Khan, the faujdar there, had a very strong army, he had ample supplies of food and ammunition and he had one of the cannons. There is a long battle, in which there are large cannons in addition to burrows and rakes. The fortifications of the city are also very strong. The Singhs, on the other hand, had only swords and spears. The Ram Jangs were very few. It was impossible to equip the Singhs with the necessary equipment for war at this time, when their resources were meager and all the enemies around them were enemies. Banda Singh's success in this situation was due to the fact that he had the maximum number of head-sucking suras who could strike the head and torso like the heroes of Chamkaur. Majhail and Doabi Singh, who were stopped across the Sutlej of Uttar Pradesh. Apart from these, the Singhs who came with Banda Singh from the South, and especially the five councilors, who were very Majhails, naturally wanted their brothers and sisters who had traveled far and wide at the behest of the Guru for centuries. They had come to the Sutlej to join the crusade against the enemy and plunder of Sirhind. With all this in mind, Banda Singh marched a long way to the east and marched towards Kiratpur.

The battle of Chappar-Chiri (Sirhand) was attended by Majheals and Doabis but great rejoicing was celebrated in Banda Singh's camp, prayers were offered to God and open mouths of Karah Prasad were distributed. The Singhs were now in a frenzy and eager to wage a crusade against Guru Mari Sirhind and his faujdar Wazir Khan. At the same time, the number of looters and looters was increasing who were staring at the looting of wealth accumulated here for centuries and were following Banda Singh's camp. Seeing this, Banda Singh ordered preparations for an invasion of the frontier. With this the waves of the Singhs began to turn more and the sky resounded with the shouts of 'Sat Sri Akal'.

At this time a Hindu officer from Sirhind, who according to the author of 'Banda di Bev' was the nephew of Nawab Wazir Khan's presenter Sucha Nand, came to Banda Singh's camp with a thousand men and said that I and my family Fed up with Wazir Khan's tyranny over the tribe, I left Sirhind and took refuge in the Khalsa for revenge and brought my loyal men with me. In fact, all this was a blot to deceive Banda Singh and he was sent by Wazir Khan and Suchanand to go to the camp of the Singhs and gain their trust and call Banda Singh across when the stakes were high. If the Singhs did not get a chance, then during the Singhs' attack on Sirhind, such a move was made that the Singhs fail. Such deceptions were not uncommon then but Banda Singh lived in the company of saints.

He relied on the story of the Sirhindi Hindu officer and allowed him to join his camp. Sirhind had been in the eyes of the Khalsas for five and a half years. In this cruel land, two innocent sons of Guru Gobind Singh were pinned to the living wall and then hacked to death in Poh Sammat 2B in December AD. It seems necessary to mention here only a hint of this horrible incident. After Guru Gobind Singh's departure from Anandpur in December AD, when the treacherous hill chiefs and the imperial forces invaded the right bank of the Sarsa and the Ropari Ranghars on the other side tried to stop him, Guru Gobind Singh was in turmoil. Singh's two youngest sons, Zoravar Singh and Fateh Singh and Mata Gujri, separated from him.

They were handed over to the Ranghar rulers of Murinda by a Brahmin named Gangu of Saheri village, one of his servants, and the Murindis handed them over to Nawab Wazir Khan of Sirhind. Wazir Khan remained an enemy of Guru Gobind Singh. He issued orders to torture these innocents and said that their lives could be spared if they became Muslims but the Sahibzada did not accept apostasy and accepted the death penalty. By the order of Nawab Wazir Khan they were subjected to all kinds of torture and intimidation . Wazir Khan was frustrated by the failure to convert two innocent children to Islam, and it seems that he may have been thinking of letting them go. 'Aafi kushtan wa bacha-sh nigah datan kari khid manda nist, aakbati gurgzada gurg shavad (That is to say, killing the snake and keeping the spools is not the work of the wise, the child of the wolf is after all a wolf), angered the Nawab.

He said to Nawab Sher Mohammad Khan Maler-Kotlia who was sitting there, "I hand them over to you. You kill them and avenge your brothers and nephews who were killed in the battle of Chamkaur. But Sher Mohammad Khan is merciful." Pathan was the son. He considered it inappropriate to take revenge on innocent children and nephews who died fighting in the war and raised his voice against this cruelty but Nawab Wazir Khan paid no heed to it and ordered the executioners to kill the Sahibzada's co-court. Be given Just what was then! The executioners with knives knocked the Sahibzada to the ground and threw him under the knees. Hearing this, the Guru's mother died in captivity in the cool tower. It was December 6, AD. (According to the new method) the cruel story of Sirhind which was inspiring Banda Singh and the Singhs to invade Sirhind. James Brown writes that "Of all the examples of persecution of preachers of new religious principles, this is the most brutal and brutal atrocity. It would not have mattered if the Sikhs were so angry. " The fear of revenge for the murders of these innocents was frightening Wazir Khan the most.

So he did his best to save himself and Sirhind and used all means! Char Panj called his fellow faujdars and big landlords for help and declared Islamic Jihad against the Sikhs in order to gather maximum number of Muslim supporters. It was too late for the jihad to begin when Wazir Khan, along with the government forces coming from far and near, gathered near Wazir Khan. He filled the corners of the gunpowder with coins and brought cannon cords and elephants to fight the Singhs. Khafi Khan puts the total number of Wazir Khan's army at Muntakhabbul-Lubab at fifteen thousand.

Banda Singh, on the other hand, had three types of men. At first he was a sincere and obedient Drid Singh, who had received the touch of Guru's feet and in whom the light of Guru Maharaj's awakened religion and sacrifice for the country was burning. Some of them had come with Banda Singh from the South and the rest had come with their heads bowed for the war of religion on the orders of Satguru. The only goal in front of these headless suras was to serve the country and religion as per the Guru's order. They had no personal interest and no greed for money or loot but hundreds of them joined hands with Banda Singh by selling their possessions to buy weapons. .The second type were the people who were recruited and sent on paid salaries by the chiefs like Phulkia etc. who for some reason could not join Banda Singh's army but their sympathy was with the Singhs and to help them in any way possible. Were eager. Thirdly, there were independent manchals who were mixed in Banda Singh's camp only with greed for booty and goods. Among them were a large number of professional looters and looters who came together to plunder the cities and towns instead of looting the streets of the merchants alone. Along with them were a few miserable peasants or other people who were at one time searching for their personal grievances and grievances. In particular, these were the people who were responsible for the looting and indiscriminate killings of the Singhs in their current campaigns.

Even in Singh's battles, it was observed many times that whenever there was a fear of defeat, these people ran away from the battle. Banda Singh had neither artillery nor elephants, nor horses for all his men. Long spears, bows and arrows and swords were all the equipment of the Singhs but the invincible courage and unwavering agility of Banda Singh and his devotees was to a large extent covering the shortfall. If he had the greatest confidence, it was the zeal and courage for the Crusades which, as soon as he saw Sirhind, would have been instilled in the minds of the Singhs by the attention of the tyrants on the Sahibzada. It is not possible to estimate the strength of the Singhs who invaded Sirhind. Khafi Khan says that the number of Sikhs was thirty to forty thousand but this number seems to have been given much more than the number of Muslims;
As soon as the news of Banda Singh's readiness to attack Sirhind reached Faujdar Khan, he himself marched from Sirhind to stop the advance of the Singhs with an army of thousands of cavalry, armored personnel carriers, archers and artillerymen and elephants. Fell On the other hand, Banda Singh also got the news of Wazir Khan's invasion and he too went for resistance.

The Sikhs came face to face with the Muslim army and quickly brought the gun fence and the battle hand to hand and the whole fist and some of his men fought so bravely that the piles of dead bodies of the infidels fell on the ground and The Day of Judgment noise was heard on all sides of the battlefield and finally the whole army of Muslims was killed and Wazir Khan was left alone. Baz Singh snatched the spear from Wazir Khan's hand and struck him on the head of his horse, injuring him.
He took it out of his furnace and struck it on Baz Singh's arm and drew his sword. He approached to kill him

The memory of the Sahibzada's assassination aroused the wrath of the Singhs. It was not easy to stop them. Beatings began in Muslim neighborhoods.

At that moment, looters looted, and the city was plundered. Upon hearing the news of his father's death and the defeat of the army, Wazir Khan's eldest son, Daulat Mall, left everything behind and fled to Delhi with his family's men.

After the capture of Sirhind, Banda Singh began to focus on the management of the conquered territories. Baz Singh, who had accompanied him from Nanded, was appointed ruler of Sirhind and Ali Singh was made his deputy. With Sirhind as its central base, troops were sent to the south, east and west to attack the malls. The Singhs had such a fear and awe on them that whether Muslims or Hindus, all government officials would be happy to accept it as soon as the Singhs arrived.

With the return of Banda Singh and other Singhs to the Punjab, and the news of their victories continued to reach Delhi, the Farrukhser emperor was alarmed and the amirs and viziers of the royal court became agitated. Abdus Samad Khan, the Nazim (subedar) of Lahore, also remained in Lahore. Probably afraid of a direct confrontation with Banda Singh or some other reason, the Bhatti landlord had set up a riot in the Lakhi forest area at this time, so he took the army and marched south. This was not a massive campaign where the Governor of Punjab needed to go himself. Emperor Farukhsiyar also did not like Abdus Samad Khan's departure for Lakhi Jungle at such a time and

when news of Banda Singh's capture of Kalanaur, Batala and Raipur reached Delhi on 5 March, the king wrote a letter of reprimand and order to Abdus Samad Wherever he went, he immediately went against Banda Singh. Prithi Chand and many other Hindu and Muslim chiefs were ordered to raise troops and go to the Punjab to assist Abdus Samad Khan. Similarly, royal licenses were issued in the name of several faujdars and jagirdars of Punjab to join Abdus Samad Khan's army with their own armies.

The order was passed . The king received news from Punjab that Sikhs were sitting in some parganas and had reached twelve kohs from Lahore city. They are running and in that place Singh is establishing his occupation and bureaucracy.

Banda Singh, on the other hand, was not at all unaware of the preparations being made in Lahore. So he decided to build a mud fort at Kot Mirza Jaan village between Batala and Kalanaur. The armies came upon the Singhs. Banda Singh held his ground in such a way that everyone was astonished and in the first battle he fought so valiantly that the royal general was about to be completely defeated and although (the royal army) He chased after him with all his might but he killed his men with such fervor and did harm to those who were lying behind him till the end. The sikhs fought so furiously that they almost overpowered the Islamic army and again and again they showed great bravery but they had no place to hide their heads, so a state of compulsion." They had to leave their places and move towards Gurdaspur. . The exact location of Banda Singh's retreat was an old village called Gurdas Nangal which has collapsed.

 Banda Singh and his companions had no choice but to take refuge in Bhidni Chand's premises (Valgan). Coincidentally, it had a very high wall around it and there was so much open space inside that all of Banda Singh's comrades could fit in there. Band ਬੰ Si ਸਿੰਘgh hastened to cook as much as he could, and did as fast as he could to stockpile food and ammunition. To keep the enemy at bay, he dug a ditch around it and filled it with water from a nearby canal. At the same time he cut through the Shah Canal and diverted water from small streams and ditches coming from the mountain which caused a swamp on all sides which could be crossed by the enemy, whether for horses or for infantry. It became difficult to be able to.

On 2nd April, the news reached King Farrukhsiar that behind Abdus Samad Khan Singhs his new Gurdas Nangal had reached its place and Are On hearing this, the emperor ordered Muhammad Amin Khan to write to Abdus Samad Khan to kill or imprison the Sikh leader (Banda Singh and his Sikh associates). When Abdus Samad Khan and his army reached Gurdas Nangal, many Singhs had gone to the villages to collect grain. As the Royal Army patrols were roaming the villages in search of Singhs, many Singhs fell into their hands. They were captured by the imperial army and tortured to death by Abdus Samad Khan.

As soon as the royal army reached Gurdas Nangal, it laid siege and closed all the checkpoints. Abdus Samad Khan had an army of 5,000 men, half cavalry and half infantry, and a large artillery. This made the siege around the Singhs so painful and made the guard so tight that not a single mound of grass and not a single grain of food could enter. On several occasions Abdus Samad Khan and his son Zakariya Khan with thousands of troops of his and his supporters tried to attack the Singhs' place but they did not succeed. A handful of Singhs defended their positions with such courage and bravery that the invaders had to turn a blind eye. Mohammad Qasim, the author of the Ibrat Nama, was present at the time in the service of Naib Nazim Arif Beg Khan of Lahore. He writes that the deeds of bravery and courage of the hellish Sikhs were astonishing. Every day two or three times some forty or fifty Sikhs would come out of the fort to graze their cattle and when the allied armies of the royal armies went to stop them they would slaughter the Mughals with their arrows, and disappear.

Now Abdus Samad Khan built high cannon fodder and pushed his front forward. The Singhs, on the other hand, continued their efforts to defend themselves and showed great courage and bravery in firing arrows and bullets at the enemy camp day and night. They would sometimes break through the siege of the imperial army and kill many. To protect their men, horses, and other livestock, the imperial army erected a ten to twenty yard long earthen embankment in front of their tents. Unbeknownst to the Singhs, they gradually filled the gaps between the bunnies with soil and filled them, thus forming a wall in front of all the tents on all sides, encircling the Singhs' fort. On several occasions, Singh bravely entered the royal compound and, overcoming all obstacles, left with whatever he could get his hands on. Baba Binod Singh would sometimes come out of the fort and return from the Imperial Lashkar Bazaar carrying sweets and other food items. The whole camp would be amazed at the courage of this old man. They tried hard to catch him but all failed. Binod Singh would have come in the evening if the army had patrolled in the morning and if he had made arrangements in the evening he would have been discharged in the evening. Each time, he slipped away from the guards. Banda singh were so brave and invincible that their enemies would applaud at their warlike qualities, and they were always afraid that the besieged Singhs would launch a single attack on them. Not only that, but the superstitious armies were convinced that Banda Singh possessed the most direct and magical powers by which he could take the form of a dog or a cat. That is why whenever they saw a dog or a cat coming from the side of the Singhs they would fall on it and as long as they did not kill it with arrows or stones they would not be satisfied.

Thus the siege and war of Gurdas Nangal continued for many months and caused great loss to both sides. Gradually the imperial forces moved forward and decided to encircle the fort of the Singhs on all sides. A thousand plowmen with axes and a thousand carpenters were employed to cut down the surrounding trees and two thousand camels were used to deliver firewood and soil.

When the circumference of the surroundings was completed, the trunks of the trees were attached to the soil by layers of soil, and the high ridges thus formed became continuously on the inside of the ridge, keeping the trench deeper and digging, thus encircling the Singhs. The siege of the surrounding ditch became more difficult to cross but in spite of all these barriers made by the besiegers, the sudden onslaught of the Singhs continued from inside which caused great loss to the outsiders. The internal defenses of the Singhs were so strong and they fired so fast and deadly from within that the imperial armies did not dare to go out in the open and attack the Singhs. Abdus Samad Khan had no hope of success against such a brave and determined enemy. All his efforts to reach the wall and door of the fort were in vain. Now the only way left for him was to reach the wall of the Singhs by digging a tunnel under the ground. So he ordered that tunnels be laid at the corners of the place. Abdus Samad Khan's tunnels had not yet reached the main gate of the citadel. Zakariya Khan then reached the other door which was used by Singh. Other faujdars and commanders also stepped up their fronts. As a result, Singh was dug up from all sides
Now the siege became so close and painful that it became impossible for the Singhs to fetch any food from outside.

The eight-month long siege had wiped them all out. Now their langar is completely gone. Not a single bait remained with them and they almost starved to death. Those who were not frightened by the enemy's cannons, guns and arrows could be frightened, they were broken by hunger. It is said that he tried to buy two or three pound grains of grain by negotiating with the imperial armies on the walls but what could have happened with this? Eventually they became very sad because of hunger.
At this time some differences arose between Baba Binod Singh and Banda Singh. It is learned that the differences arose during the deliberations on the next program. Banda Singh was not in favor of the idea that he should try to get out of here,

why he was in favor of staying here till the end, it is not known. Baba Binod Singh, on the other hand, was adamant that he should get out of here with a vengeance. As they talked, their hands went to the hilt of their swords. Seeing this, Kahan Singh, son of Baba Binod Singh, stood between his father and Banda Singh. The decision was made that whoever wants to get out of the fort should go out. Baba Binod Singh accepted the decision and rode off on horseback, tearing apart his enemies with his sword and disappearing in the twinkling of an eye.

With this the differences of opinion disappeared but there was no cure for the growing hunger pangs. The singhs finally decided to tolerate it. When there was nothing left to eat, they were forced to eat leaves of trees.

At the end of December 6, Abdus Samad Khan, as noted above, the Singhs inside were half-dead and unable to cope with illness and weakness, but the Singhs were so terrified of the imperial armies that Frightened, no one dared to go inside. Abdus Samad Khan asked the Singhs to open the door and the king vowed to ask them to forgive him but when the door was opened Banda Singh and his fellow Singhs were taken prisoner. The royal army fell on the half-dead Singh like wolves.

Banda Singh and his companions were taken to Lahore. Even though he had been captured and imprisoned, his miraculous powers were so terrifying to his enemies that they were always in danger of escaping on the road. Banda Singh had fetters on his feet, rings on his knees, chains around his waist and coils around his neck, and these were fastened with wooden rods.

Two Mughal officers were tied to the same elephant on either side of him so that he could not escape. In front of them drums and instruments were playing and the heads hanging on spears were lifted by the Mughals.

For many miles the royal road was crowded with spectators standing on either side, and the roofs of markets, streets, and mansions were lined with human-pleasing seas. Thus Abdus Samad Khan entered the city of Lahore with a procession of half-dead prisoners and blood-stained heads.

In the city of Gurdas Nangal, the royal warriors have killed everything from cats to dogs. After them was Banda Singh himself. He was bound in an iron cage and mounted on an elephant. To make fun of him, he wore a red turban on his head and a dark red robe full of pomegranate flowers. Behind him stood a naked sword-wielding officer of Muhammad Amin Khan's Turani Mughals. Behind Banda Singh's elephant were Sikh prisoners, numbering in twos, tied up in twos on two stray camels, numbered 20. On top of them were high-heeled sheepskin caps adorned with glass beads. One of his hands was attached to the neck by two screws. Some of the eminent Singhs who were walking near Banda Singh's elephant had sheepskins with their hair on the outside to make them look like bears.

Banda Singh was taken off the elephant and seated on the ground and told to either convert to Islam or be prepared for death. Instead of abandoning his religion, he accepted to sacrifice his life like a devout Sikh. Banda Singh's four year old son Ajay Singh was given his gaddi and he was told to kill him but can any father ever kill his child? He refused. What's more, the executioner cut the child to pieces with a big long knife and took out his aching heart and put it in Banda Singh's mouth.

It was Banda Singh's turn to kill. The executioner first pierced his right eye with a knife and then his left - then his left leg was amputated and behind him both his hands were amputated. With flaming red hot iron tweezers the flesh of his body was pulled and broken and finally his head was cut off and his body was cut off.

In all these painful tortures Banda Singh remain calm , he willingly gave up his life as a means to God to remove the injustices and oppressions of the time. The rest of the Singhs were treated in the same manner and all were killed.

GURU SIKHS ARE NOT SCARED OF DEATH

BOLE SONEHAL SAT SRI AKAL